Discover the
POWER
of "I AM"
Children's Mantras

Building a foundation for healthy chakras.

Written and Illustrated by:
Faith Spencer, RMT, PHD

POWER of "I AM"

Written and Illustrated by:
Faith Spencer, RMT, PHD

Published by
Joshua Tree Publishing
• Chicago •
JoshuaTreePublishing.com

All rights reserved. No part of this book may be reproduced or transmitted in any form or by any means, electronic or mechanical, including information storage and retrieval system without written permission from the publisher, except by a reviewer who may quote brief passages in a review.

13-Digit ISBN: 978-1-941049-94-5

Copyright © 2018. Faith Spencer, RMT, PhD All Rights Reserved.

Disclaimer

The information given in this book is not intended to act as a substitute for medical treatment, nor can it be used instead of mental health options. If you feel that you or your child need further help, please contact your medical doctor or call your local mental health provider. This book is to be a positive in your life but never a substitute for deeper help if needed.

It is my hope that you will continue your own understanding in natural therapies and how the can work hand in hand with western medicine.

Printed in the United States of America

DEDICATION

TO THE CHILDREN OF THIS WORLD!
You are the future and you are the light that will bring peace.
You have the POWER of I AM.

ROLE CALL
(My Kiddos)
My only Daughter **Ashley**
Oldest Son **Blake**
Middle Boy **Jeremiah**
The Baby of the Crew **Sean Riley**
You each have brought me such joy.
YOU ARE MY LIGHT!

I leave you the POWER of "I AM" so that one day you can share it with your children. This world you are in is hard, and I leave you this as a tool to help you in all stages of life. When I am not with you and you need me, read this and remember I am your number one CHEERLEADER!

Love always, MOM

SUGGESTED USE

Give your child (or yourself) the POWER of "I AM" with Mantras that are mindful and lay the foundation for healthy chakras. When you read this book with your child on a daily basis, you will empower them and allow them to process the world around them and skillfully navigate life with POWER and BALANCE. Children should have kind words that reach the subconscious and dive into their energy levels working to balance and stabilize their chakras.

This book can help CHILDREN OF ALL AGES!

CROWN

THIRD EYE

THROAT

HEART

SOLAR PLEXUS

SACRAL

ROOT

ROOT

I am safe.

I am taking responsibility for my life.

I have the power of me.

I can cope with any situation and move through the situations grounded.

I accept that the world is beyond my control, and I am taking responsibility for my life.

I need to fear less and Love More.

When I trust in myself, I build security in being me.

IMBALANCED

LOW SELF ESTEEM

LOW ENERGY

NOT GROUNDED

BALANCED

I AM CONFIDENT.

SACRAL

I am creative.

I feel good about who I am.

I have the right to talk about my desires.

I accept that not all people are
on the same level as I am.

I need to complain less and Appreciate More.

When I am grateful for what I have in my life and
who I am, I will be able to feel released.
(Free)

IMBALANCED

I HAVE LOST MY CREATIVITY.

NO SOLUTIONS TO EVERYDAY PROBLEMS.

DESPAIR.

BALANCED

I AM CREATIVE.

SOLAR PLEXUS

I am strong.

I do take the steps needed to be the
best person I can be.

I have the power to do good and change who
I am to be joyous.

I watch less and Do More.

I need to complain less and Appreciate More.

When I take an active role in my life,
I will be open to the good things in life.

IMBALANCED

FEELING ANGRY.

FEELING HELPLESS.

CANNOT FINISH TASKS.

BALANCED

I AM ORGANIZED AND CAN ACCOMPLISH MY DREAMS.

HEART

I am loved.

I will have compassion for those who
do not love themselves.

I accept that pain is part of growth.

I will love myself unconditionally for
I am good.

I need to judge less and Accept More.

Not all people can change, so I send
them into the universe with love.

IMBALANCED

I FEEL HEART BROKEN AND UNLOVED.

MY FRIENDSHIPS ARE BROKEN.

BALANCED

I AM ABLE TO LOVE and BE LOVED.

THROAT

I am expressive.

I speak truth and express my
wants in a calm manner.

When I speak in anger,
I push people away from me.

In anger I need to talk less and Listen More.

When I listen, I have the ability
to open my mind and heart.

IMBALANCED

I CAN'T EXPRESS OR EXPLAIN.

BALANCED

I AM ABLE TO EXPRESS MYSELF.

THIRD EYE

I am connected.

I see I have nothing to prove.

I make mistakes sometimes but can learn from them and grow.

I need to frown less and Smile More.

When I trust in my good,
it will allow me to find
happiness and smile.
When I smile, I have the ability to listen.

IMBALANCED

INDECISIVENESS
CONFUSION
NIGHTMARES
POOR INSIGHT

BALANCED

I AM CALM.

CROWN

I am divine. (Good)

I accept myself for who I am.

I let go of all bad thoughts
and let them go into the universe. (Sky)

I need to think less so that I can Feel More.

When I allow myself to feel, I will see.
(Connect)

IMBALANCED

FEELING ALONE
SADNESS
DEPRESSION
ANXIETY
CONFUSION
APATHY

BALANCED

I AM AT PEACE.

I AM   I AM   I AM   I AM   I AM   I AM   I AM   I AM

I have the POWER of I AM

My Personal Story
(Journey)

My children have all grown up in different ways. I am the first to admit I was not the best mother, and I can admit that it took me a long time to be aware of my shortcomings. Once I found the power of "I AM" and applied it to myself, I was able to be transformed.

I knew that I had to use it with my youngest child who is still at home with me. He suffers from many INTERNAL HIGH FREQUENCY EMOTIONS that are just too much for him to process. The tool of "I AM" has become a tool that I use and read to him daily. The little things that we can do to help our children will make an impactful difference.

So, I wanted to share my tool (this book) with the world.
WE ALL NEED HELP SOMETIMES.

About the Author

Faith Spencer, RMT, PHD has been an active practitioner of natural therapies for over 15 years. She has had wellness studios in San Diego, California, Maui, Hawaii, and now is working out of her own studio in Joshua Tree, California.

Faith has not only spent her time as a holistic health practitioner but has also enjoyed teaching Reiki and many other natural therapies across the United States and Canada. While in Hawaii, Faith and her Mother Gloria developed a healing method called Omni-Rejuvenation.

As a mother, she has continued to grow in her practice of natural therapies so that she can use them in her own home. Now that she is writing stories to give her gift to the world, she hopes that children will be able to have tools for the ups and downs of life. Her gift is spread with children's books for one and all to enjoy.

www.ingramcontent.com/pod-product-compliance
Lightning Source LLC
Chambersburg PA
CBHW050750110526
44591CB00002B/35